Learn My Language! Spanish

Spanish Words at the Post Office

By Roman Patrick

Gareth Stevens Publishing

Please visit our website, www.garethstevens.com. For a free color catalog of all our high-quality books, call toll free 1-800-542-2595 or fax 1-877-542-2596.

Library of Congress Cataloging-in-Publication Data

Patrick, Roman.
Spanish words at the post office / by Roman Patrick.
 p. cm. — (Learn my language! Spanish)
Includes index.
ISBN 978-1-4824-0353-4 (pbk.)
ISBN 978-1-4824-0354-1 (6-pack)
ISBN 978-1-4824-0350-3 (library binding)
1. Postal service — Juvenile literature. 2. Spanish language — Vocabulary – Juvenile literature. I. Patrick, Roman. II. Title.
PC4129.E5 P38 2014
468—dc23

First Edition

Published in 2014 by
Gareth Stevens Publishing
111 East 14th Street, Suite 349
New York, NY 10003

Copyright © 2014 Gareth Stevens Publishing

Designer: Sarah Liddell
Editor: Therese Shea

Photo credits: Cover, p. 1 Bloomberg/Contributor/Bloomberg/Getty Images; p. 5 Andresr/Shutterstock.com; p. 7 © iStockphoto.com/wragg; p. 9 tulpahn/Shutterstock.com; p. 11 (envelope) Triff/Shutterstock.com; p. 11 (stamp) rook 76/Shutterstock.com; pp. 13, 19 (package) Laborant/Shutterstock.com; p. 15 Mesut Dogan/Shutterstock.com; p. 17 © iStockphoto.com/bgwalker; p. 19 (postmark) astudio/Shutterstock.com; p. 21 © iStockphoto.com/dardespot.

All rights reserved. No part of this book may be reproduced in any form without permission in writing from the publisher, except by a reviewer.

Printed in the United States of America

CPSIA compliance information: Batch #CW14GS: For further information contact Gareth Stevens, New York, New York at 1-800-542-2595.

Contents

My *Abuela*. 4

The Birthday Card 6

Into the Envelope. 8

Put a Stamp on It. 10

The Birthday Gift 12

At the Post Office. 14

The Mailbox. 16

Time to Pay 18

Gracias 20

Glossary. 22

For More Information. 23

Index 24

Boldface words appear in the glossary.

My *Abuela*

Abuela is Spanish for grandmother. My *abuela* taught me *español,* or Spanish. She lives far away. I'm going to the post office to send her mail. Look in the box on each page to learn how to say the Spanish words.

grandmother = abuela (ah-BWEH-lah)

Spanish = español (ehs-pah-NYOHL)

abuela

The Birthday Card

The Spanish word for birthday is *cumpleaños*. My grandmother's *cumpleaños* is next week. I'm sending her a card, or *tarjeta*. Have you ever sent someone a *tarjeta*?

---

birthday = cumpleaños (koom-pleh-AH-nyohs)

card = tarjeta (tahr-HAY-tah)

tarjeta

Into the Envelope

After I write on the card, I put it into an **envelope**. The Spanish word for envelope is *sobre*. I write my grandmother's *dirección* on the envelope. That's Spanish for address.

envelope = sobre (SOH-breh)

address = dirección (dee-rehk-SYOHN)

dirección

Grandma
4 Park Lane
Miami, FL 33101

sobre

Put a Stamp on It

Next, I put a *timbre* on the envelope. That's Spanish for stamp. I also write a return address, or *remitente*, on the envelope. That's in case it gets sent back.

stamp = timbre (TEEM-breh)

return address = remitente (reh-mee-TEHN-tay)

timbre

Cait Caldwell
64 Spruce Street
Dover, ID 83825

remitente

Grandma
4 Park Lane
Miami, FL 33101

11

The Birthday Gift

I'm sending a **package** to my grandmother, too. The Spanish for package is *paquete*. In the package is a gift, or *regalo*. I painted a picture of the two of us!

package = paquete (pah-KAY-tay)

gift = regalo (rreh-GAH-loh)

paquete

At the Post Office

Finally, we're ready to go to the *oficina de correos*. That's Spanish for post office. I see our mail carrier there! The Spanish for mail carrier is *cartero*. I wave hello.

post office = oficina de correos (oh-fee-SEE-nah deh koh-RREH-ohs)

mail carrier = cartero (kahr-TEH-roh)

oficina de correos

The Mailbox

I put the card in the *buzón*, or mailbox. I go inside to mail the package. It's very busy. Some people have packages. Others have *cartas*. That's Spanish for letters.

mailbox = buzón (boo-SOHN)

letters = cartas (KAHR-tahs)